STUDEN

"This Bible study has grown my faith in more ways than one. It's helped me have a set time just for God. With our busy schedules, it can be hard to take time to spend with God, but this Bible study has given me a time devoted to deepening my relationship with Him. It has also helped motivate me to grow in my relationship with God. Spending time with others growing in their faith has encouraged me to grow in mine as well. This definitely goes to show how having people around you with strong faith can definitely help strengthen your own. The memory verses we memorized every week helped me come back to Scripture and spend time in God's word. I am so very thankful to Izzy, Kayla, and Olivia for being such encouraging and inspiring people with such beautiful faith."

-**Peyton**, 10th grade student

"In so many ways, my relationship with God and my small group has strengthened. I got to know God better through Scripture and be reminded of how important my relationship with Him is. This Bible study has been such a gift and I not only got to know God better, I got to know my group better as well. Putting God as my #1 priority with my small group has been the greatest gift and getting to do Bible Study with some of my best friends has reminded me about how important having friends that bring you closer to God is. I'm so so so grateful and I will cherish these meetings forever!!"

-**Kayla**, 9th grade student

"This Bible study has grown my faith because it made me very intentional about spending time with God and really made me reflect on my relationship with Him. I feel like I got to truly deepen my faith because I started to actually think of God as my best friend and a place to confide in. I got to find my confidence in Him and try things I would've never imagined I could do without Him. Throughout COVID and difficult church situations, my small group gave me a place to come back to and remember why I love God so much."

-**Olivia**, 10th *grade student*

"I have learned that even if all my hobbies, family, or anything I love is taken away, I am still a child of God and God still loves me. I'm happy that I got to do this with my best friend and my older sister. I feel like this Bible study has helped me grow my relationship with everyone and I learned so many things about myself and God that I will remind myself with every day."

-**Noelle**, 6th *grade student*

"This Bible study has taught me so much about God. It has shown me that God will always be there for me. It has helped me find my confidence and has helped me find my identity and that I am a child of God."

-**Reese**, 6th *grade student*

PARENT TESTIMONIES

"As a mother of an 11-year-old and 16-year-old daughter, my heartfelt prayer has been for them to discover and connect with God amidst the unique challenges of this modern world. *"Finding God, Finding Me"* has proven to be an invaluable resource, assuring my girls that they are not alone in their teenage struggles and that God's unwavering love meets them right where they are. The study guide, which my daughters were fortunate to go through with Izzy herself, has facilitated introspection and deepened their understanding of both themselves and God's Word. I highly recommend this study guide as a companion to *"Finding God, Finding Me"* for a heightened practical application experience."

-**Katie Luu**, Peyton and Reese's mom

"For those seeking to dive deeper into Scripture, Izzy Koo's latest study guide is the perfect companion to *"Finding God, Finding Me"*. As a parent, it was inspiring to see my daughter finding her own path to God through Izzy's study guide and leadership. As young lives have become more fast-paced than ever, finding the motivation to pause daily to seek, listen, and take in God's word is challenging. This devotional allows teens to sink into the Word in a meaningful and mindful way with intention."

-**Lauren Choi**, Kayla's mom

"The teenage years are such a critical and challenging time for many teens who struggle to fit in, be accepted, and find their identity. Izzy's first book, *"Finding God, Finding Me"*, talks about all of those fears, struggles, and insecurities. Now, with the help of her new study guide, she is able to walk you through each hardship chapter by chapter to help you find your identity and confidence in God. This is a wonderful guide and resource not only for small groups, leaders of youth, but also a perfect companion and invaluable tool for individuals to practically apply the ideas from the book to everyday life. My girls got to personally go through this study guide with Izzy as it was being written. The hands-on application of this guide brought each chapter of her book to life and I got to witness the beautiful transformation of my girls' faith throughout the summer."

-**Ashley Koo**, mom of Izzy, Olivia, and Noelle

WHAT PEOPLE ARE SAYING:

"There are so many ways for our youth and young adults to move away from finding their authentic selves and the beauty of walking with God. But I thank God for young people, like the creator of this Bible study, who are giving testimony to the Biblical voice and lessons of Ecclesiastes today: "Remember now your Creator in the days of your youth… Before the difficult days come and… While the sun and the light, the moon, and the stars, are not darkened…" Indeed, I am grateful for Ms. Izzy's work and invitation to a creative and lovely process, especially designed for youth, for doing this with the guidance of her book."

-**Rev. Dr. Angelique Walker-Smith**, *Author of Ahead of Her Time: Pan African Women of Faith and the Vision of Unity, Mission, and Justice*

FINDING YOU

8-WEEK TEEN BIBLE STUDY GUIDE

Copyright © 2024 by Izzy Koo

All rights reserved.

No portion of this book may be reproduced in any form without written permission from the publisher or author, except as permitted by U.S. copyright law.

Cover by Izzy Koo

Illustrations designed on Canva by Izzy Koo

HERE'S TO FINDING

(WRITE YOUR NAME HERE!)

ABOUT THE STUDY

Hi! My name is Izzy, and I'm currently a college student at Pepperdine University (the best school ever!!!). I made this Bible study guide for any teenager out there who is seeking God or wants to grow their relationship with Him. As a young person myself, I know how hard it is to be a Christian in today's day in age. However, God has taken me on a transformative journey to finding Him, and He has just absolutely changed my life.

I created this resource because I want your life to change too. Throughout this guide, I share my stories, inner thoughts, and revelations that have ultimately led me to where I am today as a confident young person who is on fire for God. As you embark on this journey for the next eight weeks, I hope to walk alongside you as a mentor and also as a friend. This study is filled with the questions, obstacles, and convictions God has taught me in my own journey. I hope sharing them encourages and challenges you to wrestle with these questions, obstacles, and convictions in your own, personal way.

This study guide is a supplement to my book, *"Finding God, Finding Me"*, and you will see that each chapter of my book corresponds to each meeting in this Bible study. I recommend reading each corresponding chapter of my book before starting each meeting, but feel free to also do this study as a stand-alone as well. This is the beginning of your journey to finding YOU!

WHY I CREATED THIS GUIDE

It all started with my book. I wrote *"Finding God, Finding Me"* when I was 16 years old after a radical encounter with God in my sophomore year of high school. I didn't realize it then, but I was so lucky to have had mentors and a flourishing church that provided a space for me to meet God and grow my faith. I realize for many of my friends and younger youth I know now, they don't have those same resources and people to guide them.

That breaks my heart. Our teenage years are such an important time in our lives. Most youth decide whether they want to follow Jesus or not between the ages of 13-18. Both of my two younger sisters fall around that age window, and as their older sister, all I want is for them to find Jesus and flourish in their faith. However, with an increasing lack of youth leaders and pastors who are committed to and passionate about the next generation, my sisters haven't had the mentors and transformative youth group experience I was lucky enough to have.

Well, during the summer after my first year of college, I expressed this frustration to my mom. I told her how desperately I wanted my sisters and every other youth to be poured into and invested in by leaders and people who care about them. I told her that all I wanted was for them to have every opportunity to meet Jesus.

That's when my incredible mom gave me the idea to start a small group with my sisters. The idea was to simply gather once a week for Bible study and fellowship. She told me if I truly wanted to make a difference, I should start with the youth right in front of me—my sisters, Olivia and Noelle. I thought it was a brilliant idea.

But as I looked online for a good Bible study guide for teens, I couldn't find one that I felt would really resonate with these high school girls. Most of the ones I found were too complicated, too outdated, or too far removed from the challenges and questions I knew my generation was facing. **So, I decided I would create my own**—one that was relevant, relatable, and from the perspective of a youth to another youth. I wanted to talk about the topics the girls wanted to talk about.

That's why this study was created. Knowing *"Finding God, Finding Me"* resonates with a lot of young people, I used my book as a guide as I designed this Bible study. I created the guide to be simple to follow and understand, yet rich in its meaning and applications. I made each meeting correspond to a chapter in my book to cover all the important values I found during my own journey with God. Identity. Confidence. Purpose. I wanted to dive into all of these critical topics. Once I finished writing the curriculum, I reached out to my sister's two best friends and started holding weekly Bible studies. The girls named our group >rubies – inspired by Proverbs 31:10: "She is worth far more than rubies."

The Bible study went so well with the high school girls that I started one for my middle school sister and her best friend as well. I used the same curriculum, and they got just as much out of the study.

They dove deep into Scripture together, shared vulnerably, talked about hard questions, and held each other accountable. They were inspired by the older girls and decided to call themselves the baby rubies. Both girls said that Bible study was their favorite part of the summer—how awesome is that?

This experience creating and doing a Bible study with these young girls was transformational, to say the least. I was left in awe of these girls' willingness to learn, their deep desire to search for Jesus, and their commitment to engaging with Scripture in and out of Bible study. I truly believe every youth has this willingness in them; they just need to be given a mentor and a space to explore and talk about their faith.

This Bible study guide is my attempt to provide you with that mentorship and space. Throughout this study, I will sprinkle in pictures from my meetings with my sisters and their friends to encourage you that you aren't alone in your seeking for God. I hope this resource can help you pursue your faith in a practical, engaging, and meaningful way.

So, whether you're a middle or high schooler, I challenge you to form a group and commit 8 weeks to growing your relationship with God. And for all my fellow college students and young adults out there (and parents!), I urge you to choose a few young people you want to invest in and do this Bible study with them. I think you'll find that as much as this Bible study will bless the youth you mentor, it will bless you even more.

SOME PHOTOS FROM OUR WEEKLY BIBLE STUDIES

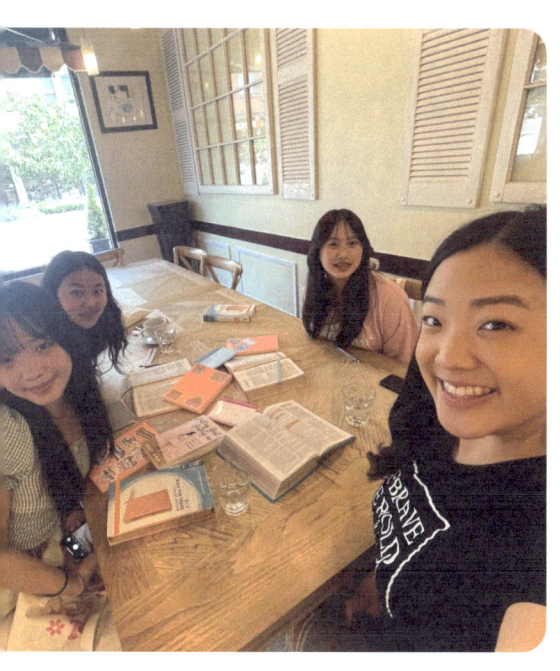

13

GROUP VS SOLO

This Bible study is designed to be done in a small group with a designated leader. Groups are great because you get to talk about these difficult and deep questions with your friends and wrestle with them together. Your group will also be able to hold you accountable, keep things fun, but most importantly, it will give you a community of friends who can encourage you because they are on the same journey. If your group can be led by a trusted mentor or slightly older friend, that's even better! Having a mentor is a game changer when it comes to growing in your faith.

With that said, this Bible study can also be done by yourself, with a friend, sibling, or parent as well. If you are doing it alone, I would highly recommend reading my book along with it—you can imagine that I am there doing it with you!

Regardless of how you choose to do this study, I urge you to go into it with an open and willing heart for God to touch your life. From one youth to another, I'm telling you that God changes everything. Your life will never be the same, and it shouldn't be the same. Finding God is just that transformative.

MATERIALS

These materials are some of my favorites when I lead this Bible study. The Bible and book are essential, and the others are optional (but highly recommended for groups!). Feel free to choose your own brands, colors, and Bible translations. However, keep in mind that the Scriptures in this guide are in the NIV translation.

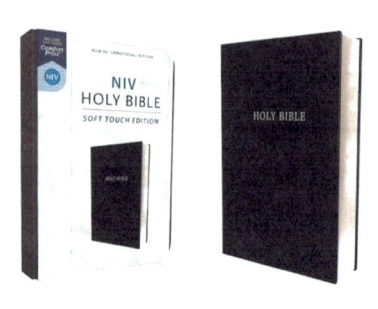

NIV Bible for Teens

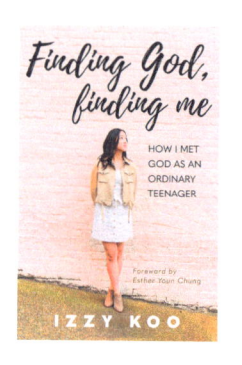

"Finding God, Finding Me" Book by Izzy Koo

Spiral Bound Index Cards

Bible Highlighters

Tote bag

Stickers to award Bible verse memory

16

MEETING 3 SUPPLIES

Meeting 3 of this study (page 51) includes a fun painting activity. This meeting is always the highlight of this entire Bible study, so make sure you prepare for this one! I got all my supplies from a local craft store near me, but you can find these materials anywhere online or at any craft store near you. Make sure you have these materials prior to Meeting 3.

WHAT TO BUY:

Acrylic Paint Set

Paintbrushes

8x8 Canvas (need one per person)

WHAT TO BRING:

- Paper cups for water (to clean brushes in-between colors)

- Water bottle to pour water into paint cups

- Paper plates for paint

- Paper towels/napkins!!

- Thin sharpie to write on canvas at the end

- Picnic blanket to sit on

- Lunch/snacks depending on when you go (I usually pick up chipotle for my group! and have everyone else bring their favorite snacks)

*I pack all my supplies in a big bag - it keeps everything together and organized :)

FOR LEADERS:

Leaders! Here are some tips and guidelines as you begin your Bible study. **Make sure to read all of this before you start!**

First of all, thank you for choosing to be a leader. Whether you feel like an expert Bible study leader or completely unprepared, you are holding this guide for a reason. You are meant to lead this study, and it will be a transformational experience for both you and your group.

BEFORE YOU START:

- When creating your group, you can do this study with as few or as many students as you'd like. However, I have found that 2-4 is the sweet spot to really get to know your group.

- Choose a space for your group! I love taking my groups to local coffee shops for our meetings. **FOR MEETING 3 - there is a painting activity, so I encourage you to take your group to a park or open space near you for that meeting.**

- Lunch/afternoon time is best for these meetings. I usually treat my girls out to lunch or coffee/drinks and then we have Bible study right afterward.

- Make your group feel special! If it fits within your budget, I encourage you to purchase all the materials on page 15 for your group. Creating a cute package with all those goodies will get your students so excited to start this Bible study with you.

TIPS FOR YOUR MEETINGS

- Before you lead each meeting, I encourage you to read the corresponding chapter in my book, *"Finding God, Finding Me"*, beforehand. Make sure to also flip through the corresponding pages in this guide before each meeting so you know how each meeting should flow (especially meeting 3!)

- This guide includes questions for students to answer. For groups, encourage each student to take some time to write down their answers and then have them share out loud with the group. Do your best to give space for each student to share. Even if they are shy, every youth desires to be heard and known by those they trust.

- While I do share my personal stories in this guide, I encourage you to also share your own experiences. Consider this guide as a springboard for your own unique insights. Remember, the students should have the opportunity to know YOU on a personal level throughout this journey.

- One of the most important parts of this study is the fellowship aspect. Before you start each meeting, spend the first hour (yes, the whole hour!) catching up and simply being a friend to your group members. This is where the magic happens - where you become a friend as much as you become a mentor. The next hour should then be spent on the material in this Bible study. Thus, two hours is the perfect sweet spot for these meetings - one hour in fellowship and one hour in study.

- Keep a group chat with your group! Text your group throughout the week to see how they are doing. Attend their sports games, take each member out individually once if you can, and be there for them. Most importantly, pray for them and with them.

SCHEDULE

■	WEEK 1	**FINING GOD...............23**
■	WEEK 2	**FINDING IDENTITY.......37**
■	WEEK 3	**FINDING CONFIDENCE..51**
■	WEEK 4	**FINDING PATIENCE.....69**
■	WEEK 5	**FINDING PURPOSE.......81**
■	WEEK 6	**FINDING PASSION........93**
■	WEEK 7	**FINDING HUMILITY.....105**
■	WEEK 8	**FINDING ME...............119**

DATE:

WEEK 1
FINDING GOD

Welcome to week 1! Today, we begin with the first chapter of my book, "Finding God". It's crucial we begin with finding God because before we talk about anything else, like identity or confidence, we must first talk about the source of where all those things come from.

OUR FIRST MEETING

> The question that started my faith journey was, **"Why are you Christian?"** My dad asked me this one day at the dinner table, and it really stumped me. I had no idea why I was a Christian besides the fact that my parents were and that I simply grew up in a Christian household. I remember telling my dad these two reasons, but he wasn't satisfied. He wanted to know specifically **why I was a Christian**. He wanted to know what God had done in my life to make *me* believe.

Well, I'm going to ask you the same question. Why are **YOU** Christian? What is **YOUR** reason for believing in God?

it's ok if you don't know!

_____

_____
_____
_____
_____
_____
_____
_____

It's completely okay if you don't have a solid answer yet. I had no idea what to say at the time. However, not knowing why I was Christian led me to be tempted on many occasions not to be a Christian anymore because **my beliefs weren't rooted in a strong foundation**. I was always swayed by my friends' unbelief and wanted to fit in with the secular culture in order to not stand out. Being a Christian is not always the most popular thing to be. In fact, it's so **hard** to be a Christian in our world today.

That's why it's critical to know why you believe.

I eventually got to a point where I was so frustrated because I didn't know why I believed in God. My faith had always been a label I wore rather than something I truly lived out or believed. At the time, I wondered if I even believed at all. Can you relate to this? Is your faith just a **label** or a **way of life** for you?

_____

_____

_____

_____

_____

For me, my faith had always been a label. Besides going to church on Sundays, there was nothing else I did that made me Christian. I was a follower of God because that's all I knew. I didn't actually have my own relationship with God. So, I began a search for God. I stayed up all night reading the Bible and tried praying for long periods of time. I wanted to see if God was Someone I truly wanted to believe in **for myself.**

Has there been a time in your life when you intentionally searched like this for God?

_____

_____

_____

If you're like me and you haven't, this Bible study is the perfect chance for you to do so. It was through intentionally seeking God and seeking truth that I came to find Him.

Turn to Matthew 7:7-8 in your Bible

> "Ask and it will be given to you; seek and you will find; knock and the door will be opened to you. For everyone who asks receives; **the one who seeks finds**; and to the one who knocks, the door will be opened." - Matthew 7:7-8

what stands out?

_____

_____

_____

All God asks of you is to seek Him because when you do, you will find Him. I have always been fascinated by this verse because of its confidence. It doesn't just say that some of those who ask will receive – it says all who ask will receive. **I am a living testimony of this.**

As someone who is now on the other side of the open door, I can tell you that God is a God of keeping His promises. Just a few years back, when I was 16, God met me, and my life completely changed.

God met me when I was the most broken and lonely version of myself. I felt like everything I loved had been taken away from me, and it was at this point of complete and utter desperation that God surrounded me with His overwhelming love. He met me when I realized I had nothing except for God. Through a transformational and emotional encounter, I realized how much I'm loved by Him.

Do you feel like you have found God yet?

Before answering that question, keep in mind that "finding God" doesn't mean you had to have an emotional encounter like me. God meets people in all sorts of ways. For example, my dad met God one day while walking outside. He looked at the beautiful nature and said to himself, "There has to be a God who created this." My question to you is: **Have you had a moment in your life where you met God in a personal way?**

_____

_____

_____

_____

Maybe you've had your "encounter" moment with God, and perhaps you haven't. Over the years, I've learned that God meets you when you understand that He is the only one who can fill your emptiness and loneliness, and you surrender completely to Him. **This heart posture is where you find God.**

I've also found that God meets everyone with the same truth – just in unique ways according to your personality, circumstances, and perspectives. However, the truth of the Gospel is always the same. I know you've probably heard it a million times before, but there will be a time (or maybe you've had it already) when you understand and accept this truth in the deepest part of your heart:

> **God loves you so much that He sent His son Jesus to die on a cross for your sins so that you can enjoy everlasting life with God in Heaven. No matter what you've done, what you've thought, or what you feel like you deserve, God has forgiven every wrong you've committed and will commit, and He calls you His son and daughter. You are a child of God, and He says you are worthy of love.**

I hope that as we go through this study, this truth of the Gospel will sink into the deepest part of your heart. So don't worry if you haven't fully found God yet—**that's what this Bible study is for**. With each meeting, you will learn more about God and get to know Him better. Also, seeking and finding God isn't just a one-time action. It's something even mature believers have to do on a daily basis. We are always seeking and finding God in different ways. That's the beauty of walking with Him.

The important thing is to have someone to walk with during your faith journey. I was lucky enough to have a brilliant **mentor** named Pastor Esther. Pastor Esther was my youth pastor and the person God used to lead me to Him. Not only that, after I met God, Pastor Esther met with me once a week at the same coffee shop for *two years*. During our weekly meetings, she let me share about everything God was teaching me and encouraged me to be everything God created me to be. I am where I am today in my faith because of her mentorship.

Do you have a mentor in your life? If not mentors, do you have people you can talk about your faith with and ask questions to?

_____

_____

_____

_____

_____

Mentors are everything – I believe every teenager needs a mentor. **We need people in our lives who both challenge us and speak life into us.** If you don't have a mentor, I would encourage you to look for an older sister or brother figure in your life who's a couple of years older and that you look up to spiritually. Ask them if they'd be willing to meet with you regularly to talk and confide in. I promise you – **having a mentor changes everything**.

But with a mentor or not, this study is for you to find your own relationship with Jesus. Whether you've been walking with Jesus for a while or just beginning your journey, **let today be the start of a new search for God and meeting Him in a new way**.

What are **two practical action items** you can do this week to seek God more in your life? (Ex: reading your Bible once a day, praying more intentional prayers, worshiping before bed, listening to a sermon)

1 _____

2 _____

MEMORY VERSES!

Each week, there will be a memory verse to memorize. And no, it's not because it's a "Bible study" thing to do. I've genuinely seen how keeping God's word in my heart and mind has **changed my life**. Memorizing Scripture is so powerful because it reminds you of God's truth when you feel the most tested, defeated, and weak. It also helps you answer people when they ask about your faith. For example, if someone asks why you read your Bible, you can respond, "It's because Matthew 7:7 says that when you seek God, you will find Him!"

This week's verses are **Matthew 7:7-8**. If you have a spiral notepad (one of the recommended materials), you can start writing these weekly verses on there—it makes it super helpful to memorize. If not, you can write them down on notecards and place them somewhere you can see them every day.

"Ask and it will be given to you; seek and you will find; knock and the door will be opened to you. For everyone who asks receives; **the one who seeks finds**; and to the one who knocks, the door will be opened." - Matthew 7:7-8

If you're in a group, your leader should have everyone recite each week's verse at the beginning of each meeting. I usually award stickers per verse memorized (hey, stickers are cool!). **Keep all these verses in your memory.** There will be a final challenge during the last meeting to see who can recite all eight verses at once!

That's it for week 1! This is the beginning of an exciting journey. I know that God is going to meet you in a special and new way during these next eight weeks. Keep seeking Him and knocking on His door because He is waiting for you with so much joy on the other side. There will always be a space to write your **prayer requests** for the week after each meeting. I encourage you to look back each week and see how God answers your prayers.

PRAYER REQUESTS

DATE:

Recite Matthew 7:7-8

WEEK 2
FINDING IDENTITY

Hello hello! It's time to talk about identity. I feel like identity gets brought up a lot these days. We all want to know who we are and be firmly grounded in what that is. It seems like everyone is known for something, so naturally, we are constantly trying to find our "thing" we want to be known for.

Here's an example: You are describing someone to your friend. When you're trying to describe someone to your friend, you are identifying them through **identifiers**. You might say something like, "He's the band kid" or "She's the one who's really good at basketball." We describe people by associating them with some "thing." There are all sorts of "things" to identify people by:

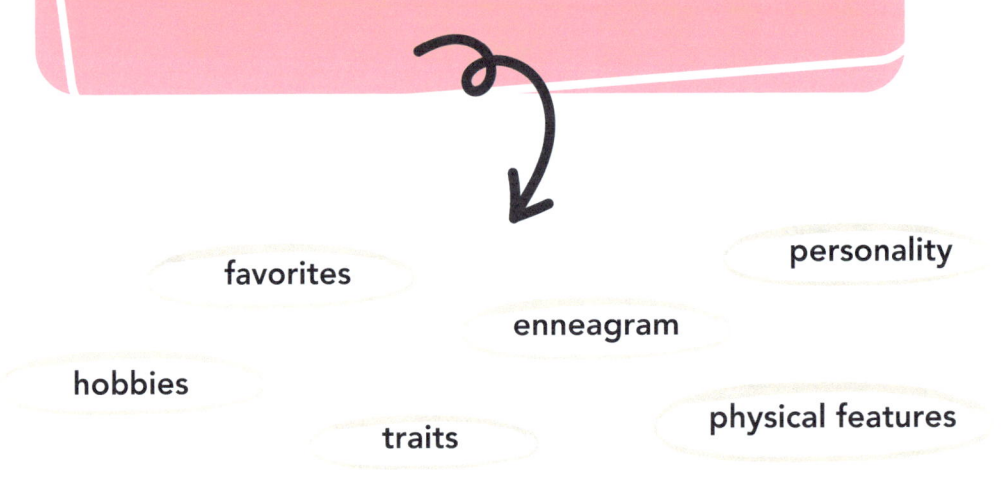

favorites

personality

enneagram

hobbies

physical features

traits

What are your identifiers? For example, if your classmate were to describe you to someone, **how do you think they would describe you?**

_____

_____

_____

_____

For me, I was always described as "the volleyball girl." Volleyball was **EVERYTHING** to me - you could say I was obsessed. I practiced every day in my backyard, attended all the extra practice sessions I could, watched YouTube videos to get better, and constantly dreamed of becoming a professional volleyball player. I literally had those "volleyball is life" stickers all over my water bottles and binders - **I truly believed volleyball was my identity**.

> **My sport became who I believed I was.**

The scary part was that because volleyball became my identity, my happiness and mood depended on whether I was doing well or poorly at practice. I would be overjoyed when I was doing well, but I would be devastated and crushed if I wasn't. That devastation often made me think I was **less worthy** if I wasn't excelling at volleyball.

Isn't that crazy? I let the sport I played determine my value and what I believed I was worth. Because of that, I was never at peace. I was constantly worried about my performance and "doing well." I allowed those thoughts to consume my mind so much.

This led me down an unhealthy cycle of always seeking affirmation, validation, and success. The worst part was that the place I was seeking this from was very fickle and ever-changing. I couldn't always control how well I played. So, in the end, **volleyball started controlling me**.

Do you have something in your life **determining** your happiness or feelings of self-worth? Tell me about it.

_____

_____

_____

_____

_____

_____

_____

Whatever your "volleyball" is, I think we can both agree that it's exhausting having your identity tied to something as fickle as a hobby. **I always felt like I had to prove myself to people.** I felt like I had to constantly succeed and do well to be respected, celebrated, and acknowledged by others. Because of that, **I thought I would be nothing if I didn't have volleyball**.

have you ever felt like this before?

Let's do an exercise.

I want you to write your name in the center of the circle and draw multiple lines out of the circle just like the one already done. Each extension should have a circle with a word representing a part of who you are (think about your associations from earlier).

> some words I used were "volleyball," "sister," "Asian-American," and "writer"

student

Now, I want you to go back to the previous page and cross off all your extensions except for your **top 3.** List them here:

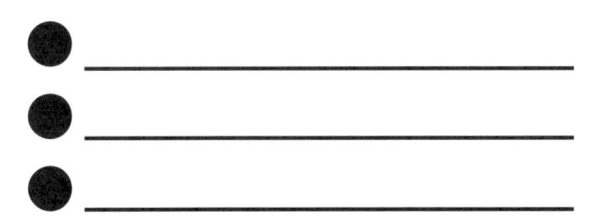

- _____
- _____
- _____

Now, go back and cross off two more extensions to narrow it down to **just 1** - this is probably where your identity lies the most. Write down your last extension:

_____

Ok, this is the last one, I promise. Go back one more time and cross off your last extension. All of your extensions should be crossed off by now. **So, what's left?**

You'll see that **you** are still left. Even when everything is crossed out and taken away from you, **you are still left**. Your name is still written in that circle. That can only mean one thing: all those words you crossed off are not your true identity. Even without all those associations, **you are still whole and complete** (that's what the circle symbolizes). All your words in those smaller circles are gifts; they are positions of influence, talents, and passions that God has gifted you with. But if your identity is in them, you will always be disappointed.

So, where is our identity supposed to be? I realized the best place for my identity is in the **God** who created me—**the one who gave me my name that is in the circle**.

I was a slave to volleyball and all my other associations until God showed me what it looked like to have my identity in Him. **I realized that you don't have to prove anything to God. God loves you and accepts you not only when you're thriving but also when you're at your worst. God is proud of you. You are more than good enough for God. His love for you doesn't depend on how well you do or how many awards you win.**

The only secure and solid place for you to put your identity in is God. When your identity is in God, you will be rooted in a firm foundation on which you can build your whole life confidently and purposefully.

Turn to Romans 8:38-39

> "For I am convinced that neither death nor life, neither angels nor demons, neither the present nor the future, nor any powers, neither height nor depth, nor anything else in all creation, will be able to separate us from the love of God that is in Christ Jesus our Lord."

what stands out?

_____

_____

_____

Not even **death** can separate you from the love God has for you. Do you know what that means? A bad test score, game, or even moral slip-up can't make God love you any less. How freeing and comforting is that!

After discovering God's unconditional love for me, I realized I wanted my identity to be in Him. **I wanted my identity to be in something secure, solid, and unchangeable. Only God can provide that.**

But what exactly does it mean to have your identity in God? It means that we are who *God* says we are. **Well, who does God say that we are?**

> "See what great love the Father has lavished on us, that we should be called **children of God! And that is what we are!** The reason the world does not know us is that it did not know him." – 1 John 3:1

> "But you are a **chosen** people, a **royal** priesthood, a **holy** nation, God's **special possession**, that you may declare the praises of him who called you out of darkness into his **wonderful light**." – 1 Peter 2:9

note:

In 1 Peter 2:9, Peter describes God's special relationship with Israel as His chosen race. However, as Christians, **we are also a chosen spiritual race by God**. We are called out and set apart from everyone else as believers in Jesus.

From those two verses alone, God clearly tells us about our identity. **We are chosen, royal, holy, special, God's possession, people called from darkness into wonderful light, and children of God. That is who we are.**

Does knowing this about your identity give you any comfort? Does it relieve any burden? Is it hard to accept this as your identity? Is it easy?

_____

_____

_____

_____

_____

> I hope you can accept these words as your identity today and every day. You are who God says you are, and God says you are his chosen child. **Nothing and no one can take that away from you.**

This week's memory verse is either **1 John 3:1** or **1 Peter 2:9**. Memorize the one that spoke to you more, and keep it in the back of your mind to pull out whenever you lose sight of who you are. I love 1 Peter 2:9.

"But you are a **chosen** people, a **royal** priesthood, a **holy** nation, **God's special possession**, that you may declare the praises of him who called you out of darkness into his **wonderful light**." – 1 Peter 2:9

You are a child of God—remember that. That wraps up our second meeting! I hope you go into the rest of your day with a deeper and richer understanding of who you are, but more importantly, **whose you are**.

⭐ **Leaders and those doing this study by yourself: Turn to page 17 to prepare supplies for the next meeting! Refer to page 18 for directions on location for Meeting 3.**

PRAYER REQUESTS

NOTES

DATE:

Recite 1 John 3:1 or
1 Peter 2:9

⭐ *Make sure you have your supplies prepared!*

WEEK 3
FINDING CONFIDENCE

It's week 3, and this week's meeting might just be my favorite. The youth I do this Bible study with love this week the most as well. There's a painting activity planned for today to put our confidence into action. Don't worry—whether you're a skilled artist or a stick-figure-er, you will find this activity memorable and perhaps even transformative.

Alright, but before we begin our painting activity, let's first learn about confidence. The Bible study portion of today's meeting will be slightly shorter, so we have time for the activity. I will start by asking you some questions about confidence to see where you are at.

How confident would you say you are on a **scale from 1-10**?

1 2 3 4 5 6 7 8 9 10

If I were to answer this question just a few years ago, I would've circled "0". I don't think I would've even been at a "1". I was the shyest, most introverted, and closed-off person ever. I was scared to death of public speaking, interactions with new people, and even asking a waiter at a restaurant for napkins. It was that bad... anyway, next question...

When do you feel the **most** confident? When do you feel the **least** confident?

_____

_____

_____

_____

_____

Think about **the most confident person you know**. What makes them so confident?

_____

_____

_____

_____

_____

_____

> The most confident person I know was my mentor, Pastor Esther. I used to give Pastor Esther compliments all the time. I would always tell her how amazing, wise, and encouraging she was, and the funny thing is that she responded the same way every time. Pastor Esther always responded with, **"I know I am!"** However, for some reason, she never sounded arrogant when she said that. Rather, I could tell that Pastor Esther was simply so confident in who God made her to be and the gifts He gave her.

Over time, I realized that Pastor Esther's confidence never came from herself. It came from her confidence in God. She knew who God made her to be, and that was who she was confident in—the person she was because of God. The same became true for me as well. Even though I felt like I had so many weaknesses and was just so shy, I found I could rest and rely on God's strength. **I realized I could put my confidence in Him instead of myself.**

Turn to 1 Corinthians 12:9-10

> "My grace is sufficient for you, for my power is made perfect in weakness. Therefore I will boast all the more gladly about my weaknesses, so that Christ's power may rest on me. That is why, for Christ's sake, I delight in weaknesses, in insults, in hardships, in persecutions, in difficulties. For when I am weak, then I am strong."

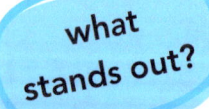

what stands out?

_____

_____

_____

God's power is made perfect in our weakness. It seems like it doesn't make sense, but that's the reality of who our God is. Even in our weakness, and **especially in our weakness**, God's power shines all the brighter.

I encourage you to read all of 1 Corinthians 12 in your own time because it is so richly packed with Paul's experience of confidence despite his shortcomings. We can learn from Paul that our weaknesses and fears shouldn't stop us from being confident. Rather, God's power is more evident in our weaknesses because it shows that God is the one working through us. **True confidence shouldn't lie in our abilities or talents. It should lie in God because it's God who makes us strong and capable.**

Note: You may have read about my rainbow loom cross story in this chapter of my book. I was so scared when I had to give that cross to the man at the burger restaurant. It was only because I trusted in God's power to transform rather than dwell on my shyness that I could give him the cross. And look what God was able to do through my "yes"!

NOTES

Now it's time to paint!

If you're with your group, you are probably sitting at a park, coffee shop, or wherever your leader decided to take you today. Your leader will guide you through today's activity. If you are by yourself or with a friend, grab your painting supplies and head to your favorite public spot (if you're not already there!). It's time to exercise some Godly confidence. Today, you will share God's love with a new friend through a simple painting.

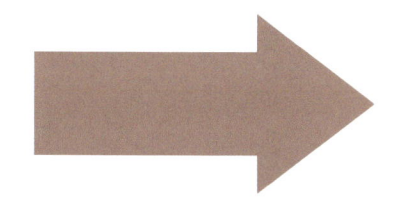

Here are some photos of my very first small groups doing this painting activity!

The >rubies - Kayla, Olivia, and Peyton (and me!)

The baby rubies - Noelle and Reese

finished products!!

"Be strong and courageous" - Joshua 1:9

"You are beautiful beyond measure" - Psalm 139:14

"You are a light in this world" - Matthew 5:14

"You are fearfully and wonderfully made" - Psalm 139:14

59

finished products!!

"Even the darkest night will end and the sun will rise" - Psalm 30:5

"Stay hopeful, stay positive" - Romans 15:13

Now it's your turn!

Get out your canvas and paint brushes! Think of an encouraging phrase to write on your canvas. I advise you not to write a Bible verse word for word because that might make the person receiving it uncomfortable if they aren't a Christian. Instead, choose a phrase that **relates** to a Bible verse but is encouraging to anyone who receives it. You will still write the Bible verse reference it relates to at the bottom of your painting. Look at the previous pages for examples and inspiration!

> Paint away and then set your canvas out to dry

When your painting completes drying, flip it over. Take a thin sharpie or pen and write a note of encouragement along the edge of the backside of your canvas. You can write whatever you would like, but I encourage you to end your message with, **"I want you to know God loves you so much."**

Once you are done, whether you are with a group, by yourself, or with a friend, take a few minutes to **pray** over your painting (out loud if you're with a group!). Pray that God would lead you to give it to someone who needs to hear your message today. Pray that God would use your painting to lead the person you give it to closer to Jesus. **This is the most crucial step in this whole activity.**

After you pray

It's time to give your painting away now. If you're nervous, that's completely normal. This is a bold and scary thing to do, but know that you will be planting a seed of faith in someone that lasts for eternity. Be confident in what you learned today about God showing up in your weakness. And know that part of life as a lover of God is to share that love with others. Jesus's final instruction to us in Matthew was this:

> "Therefore **go and make disciples of all nations**, baptizing them in the name of the Father and of the Son and of the Holy Spirit, and teaching them to obey everything I have commanded you." - Matthew 28:19

Sounds kinda scary now that you will actually be doing this, right? Well, look what Jesus writes right after the previous verse:

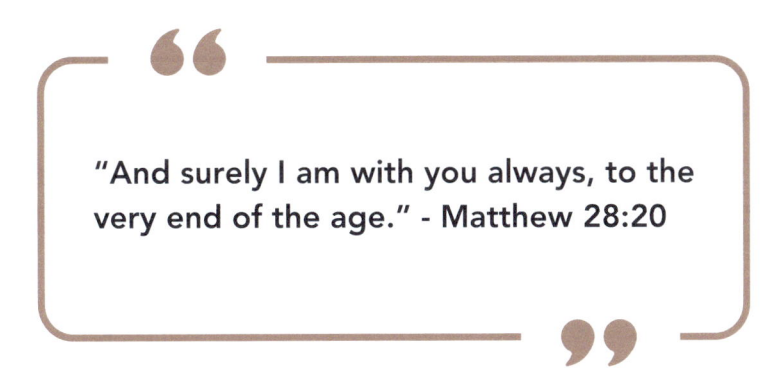

> "And surely I am with you always, to the very end of the age." - Matthew 28:20

God is with you always. He was with the disciples when He gave out this instruction, and He is with you now as you carry out His same mission. Let that sink in.

Once you're ready, walk around the park or place you're at until you find someone you want to give your painting to. Tell them about the message on your painting, and if they are receiving it well, you can even tell them about God! **You got this.**

REFLECTION QUESTIONS

What encouraging phrase did you paint on your canvas? **Why did you choose that phrase?**

_____

_____

_____

_____

_____

_____

How did it feel to give out your painting? Describe what happened.

_____

_____

_____

_____

_____

_____

I'm so proud of you. I wish I was there to witness you give your painting away in person, but truly, I want you to know that you did an extraordinary thing today. Whether the person you gave your painting to loved it or didn't, you have done your part. Now, it's up to God to do the transforming work in the person you gave it to.

This week's memory verse is either **2 Corinthians 12:9** or **Matthew 28:19**. If you need more reminders of God's strength and power, memorize 2 Corinthians 12:9. If you feel like you have the confidence but need reminders to use your confidence to share about God, memorize Matthew 28:19.

"Therefore go and make disciples of all nations, baptizing them in the name of the Father and of the Son and of the Holy Spirit." - Matthew 28:19

PRAYER REQUESTS

NOTES

DATE:

Recite 2 Corinthians 12:9 or Matthew 28:19

WEEK 4
FINDING PATIENCE

Can you believe we've already made it halfway through this study? Today's meeting is about patience. Honestly, I think one of the hardest virtues is patience. With patience, you are responding to someone else's behavior. Patience requires holding back sometimes, refraining from lashing out, and truly seeing the other person as God sees them.

I used to struggle with patience a lot—especially with my youngest sister, Noelle. We have a 10-year age gap, so when I was 16, she was only 6 years old. As you can probably imagine, when I was my grumpy and irritable high school self and had a long day at school, it did not excite me to see Noelle jumping up and down asking me to play mermaids with her when I got home.

Who is the person you have the **hardest time** showing patience to, and **why?**

_____

_____

_____

_____

_____

Over time, my patience worsened, and my relationship with Noelle did as well. I lashed out easily and often, pushed Noelle away day after day, and was bitter toward her for no reason. Reflecting on it now, I realize that I saw Noelle as a **burden** to me. I saw her as an inconvenience, and that was all I could see her as at the time. **My perception of her was so negative.**

Because I viewed Noelle as a burden, that's all I could see her as. So, of course, I would get easily upset and frustrated with her. It was because of the way I saw her. My perception was **clouded** by my decision to view my sister as an annoyance rather than as a beautiful child of God.

> I want you to think about the person you said was the hardest to show patience to. **Who is that person to you?** Sure, they might be a friend, sibling, parent, or classmate, but I want you to dig deeper – what is your **perception** of them? Is it positive or negative?

_____

_____

_____

_____

What God has taught me during my long journey to patience is that perception is everything. **You can't show patience to someone until you change your perception of them.** Since I viewed Noelle as a burden to me, how could I love her in the way I would if I viewed her as adorable?

My distorted view of Noelle caused my reactions and actions toward her to always go first to anger and irritation. **That's the power that perception has.** If it's negative, it clouds you only to see the bad in people. For me, it caused me to never even give a relationship with my sister a chance.

It's interesting because we often view other people negatively but **accept God's radically loving view of us**. We love talking about how God views us as his wonderful and beautiful creation, how God calls us royal and chosen, and how we were intricately and intentionally woven together in our mothers' wombs. Think about what we learned two weeks ago about identity. We learned from 1 Peter 2:9 that God calls us **a chosen people, a royal priesthood, a holy nation, God's special possession, and people living in wonderful light**.

We love to accept that truth for our own lives, but **do we extend that same truth to the lives of the people we struggle to love?**

I want you to write your name on the blank below and read the sentence out loud:

_____ is: **chosen, royal, holy, God's special possession, wonderful light, and a child of God**

Doesn't reading that statement about yourself feel good? It should—-you are all those things God says about you in 1 Peter. But now, I want you to fill in the next blank with **the name of the person you struggle to show patience to.** Now read that statement out loud.

_____ is: **chosen, royal, holy, God's special possession, wonderful light, and a child of God**

The same words you learned that apply to you also apply to the person you struggle to love. God sees that person as beautiful, worthy, and chosen—**just as much as you.**

How did reading that statement out loud feel? Was it hard? **Did it make you think of the person you wrote down differently?**

_____

_____

_____

_____

> When you recite 1 Peter 2:9 from now on, **I want you to remember the person you chose**. Let that verse always be a reminder not only of how God sees you but also of how God sees others.

The key to finding patience is changing your perception. If you choose to see people as beautiful, full of light, and as God's precious children, **how you treat them will change because the way you see them is changed.**

Turn to 1 Corinthians 13:4-7

> "Love is patient, love is kind. It does not envy, it does not boast, it is not proud. It does not dishonor others, it is not self-seeking, it is not easily angered, it keeps no record of wrongs. Love does not delight in evil but rejoices with the truth. It always protects, always trusts, always hopes, always perseveres."

what stands out?

In the entire chapter of 1 Corinthians 13, Paul explains beautifully and poetically about what love is. In verse 4, he writes: "Love is **patient**, love is kind. It does not envy, it does not boast, it is not proud." He then goes on to list a bunch of other attributes of love.

But isn't it interesting how the first word he uses to describe love is patience? It's almost as if he's saying that **love is patient before it is anything else**.

I had to learn how to be patient with Noelle before I could truly love her. It was only after I saw my sister the way God sees her that I was **able to change my heart and actions** toward her. Noelle is now one of my best friends and I think she's pretty incredible. I love her.

To wrap up this meeting, I want you to write **a note of praise and encouragement** to the person you have the hardest time showing patience to. Write about their good traits, what you like about them, and how incredible they are – to you and God.

NOTE OF PRAISE

_____

_____

_____

_____

_____

_____

_____

_____

_____

Your challenge this week is to **give your note to the person you wrote it for**. Read it aloud to them, or text it to them instead if that's too much. As much as the person you tell your message to will appreciate it, you will find yourself loving the person more within your heart as well.

This week's memory verse is **1 Corinthians 13:4**. This verse has convicted me on so many occasions. In my most impatient and frustrated moments, it has popped into my head and reminded me to be patient and kind. It will do the same for you.

"Love is patient, love is kind. It does not envy, it does not boast, it is not proud." - 1 Corinthians 13:4

I hope you are encouraged to go into your week with patience and love today. **Remember that everyone you meet**—from your best friend to your parents, to the stranger on the street, to your worst enemy—**is a beautiful child of God worthy of love**.

PRAYER REQUESTS

NOELLE IS PRAYING RIGHT ALONGSIDE YOU!

DATE:

Recite 1 Corinthians 13:4

WEEK 5
FINDING PURPOSE

Welcome to week 5! Today, we will talk about purpose and how important it is to know your purpose. Your "why" behind everything you do is foundational to your motivation and discernment. A strong and confident sense of purpose gives you a reason to wake up excitedly every morning and live your life with joy and hope.

When I used to think about "purpose," I immediately thought about my dream career or my ideal job. I thought about what I wanted to do with my life professionally and career-wise. I thought my answer to what my dream job was would be what my purpose was.

As you know from the meeting on identity, I was really into volleyball in middle and high school. At that time when volleyball was everything to me, **I thought my "purpose" in life was to become a great volleyball player.** I had dreams of playing collegiate and even professional volleyball.

But the thing is, my "purpose" was always changing. Throughout my childhood, I went from wanting to become a famous artist to a singer, to a graphic designer, to a professional basketball player or volleyball player, and the list goes on. **Whenever I went through a change in my dream career, I viewed it as my purpose changing.**

What comes to your mind when you think of the word **"purpose"**? What is your definition of it?

_____

_____

_____

> According to Oxford Languages, the *definition of purpose* is:
>
> **the reason for which something is done, or one's intention.**

I found out much later in life that I had gotten the definition of purpose all wrong. I realized that purpose is not what you do or what you want to do – **rather, it's why you want to do it**.

While I was playing volleyball, volleyball itself was not my purpose. My purpose was wanting to win praise, affirmation, and approval for myself. **My purpose was to glorify me.** That was the reason behind everything I did.

What is your **dream job**?

_____

I want you to think about this dream job of yours. **Why** do you want to pursue this job? What is your **purpose** for pursuing it?

_____
_____
_____
_____
_____

When I found God, I realized our true purpose should be to glorify God. If it's anything else, we will never feel we are living our lives to the freest and fullest. My purpose in life used to be **a desire to win praise and approval**.

But when I shifted my purpose from wanting to glorify myself to wanting to glorify God, **my life went from being all about me to being all about God**—and that's what has freed me and fulfilled me in a way nothing else ever has.

Now, I want everything I do to make God's name known to the world instead of my own. I want people to know about *God's* love, compassion, mercy, forgiveness, and promise of salvation. Why is this so meaningful?

By telling people about God's promise of salvation, I am planting seeds that will last for eternity. **When God becomes your "why", everything you do starts having meaning.** Everything begins to feel like you are doing something truly worth all your time, effort, and life.

Do you want God to be your "why"?

_____

Let me warn you though: a life dedicated to glorifying God will look different than the lives your non-Christian friends are living. In a world where most people our age are partying, studying like their life depends on it, stuck in constant moodiness and pessimism, and approaching life with a more or less "just get through it" attitude, **a life with Jesus as your purpose looks completely different—and it should look different.**

Our purpose to love God and love others should lead us to live a **radically different life**—a life that causes other people to look at us and wonder why we are the way we are. We should be overflowing with joy and happiness, engaging people with smiles, forgiving seventy times seven, and welcoming others with open arms. **We should be the evidence that God lives in us every single day.**

Turn to Romans 12:2

> "Do not be conformed to the pattern of this world, but be transformed by the renewing of your mind. Then you will be able to test and approve what God's will is—his good, pleasing and perfect will."

what stands out?

Paul explains true worship of God in this way in Romans 12:2. It's so easy to try to fit in with our friends and the culture. It's so easy to get caught up in the desire to live for yourself and make yourself great. But God's love is transformative.

If you call yourself a Christian, **you are called to live a transformed life.** Think about your life right now. Are you living a life that looks like it's been **transformed** by God? Are you living **radically different**?

Jesus lived a radically different life Himself. Read **Matthew 20:28** and **Philippians 2:5-8**. Both verses talk about how Jesus came into this world not to be served like everyone thought, but to serve others. Serving and loving God and people was Jesus's purpose in life. Because of His purpose, He lived a radical life that was countercultural to the world.

Does the idea of living a radically different life **scare** you? Does it **excite** you? How does it make you **feel**?

_____

_____

_____

_____

It's normal for it to seem scary. As a teenager, the most terrifying thing for me was to be seen as different from everyone else. But I'm telling you, God is worth it. **I'd rather live in complete freedom and fulfillment than live to fit in.** So, to help you reach the confidence you need, I want you to write out the "why" you want to live by. In other words, what will the purpose of your life be? **What do you want to live for?**

YOUR "WHY"

To finish up today's meeting, I want to leave you with one of my favorite quotes of all time. It's by C.S. Lewis, and it's this:

> "Christianity, if false, is of no importance, and if true, of infinite importance, the only thing it cannot be is moderately important."

If you believe Christianity to be true, God can't just be a part of your life. He just can't. To believe God is real is to believe that there is a God who created you and sent His Son to die for you and rise again from the dead so you can have the gift of eternal life with God in Heaven. To believe in God is to believe all the truths of the Bible that tell you that God is always with you and will unconditionally love you. **To believe all of that and remain the same is not possible.**

I say all this **to urge you to be confident in your "why".** Be confident in your purpose. Be confident that God is worth dedicating your whole life to. Know why you are here and how important and purposeful your life was made to be.

This week's Bible verse is **Romans 12:2**. Allow this verse to serve as a reminder not to follow the patterns of this world but to live a life radically different from it. **Our God is a God who transforms.**

"Do not be conformed to the pattern of this world, but be transformed by the renewing of your mind. Then you will be able to test and approve what God's will is—his good, pleasing and perfect will."

PRAYER REQUESTS

DATE:

Recite Romans 12:2

WEEK 6
FINDING PASSION

It's time to talk about passion. Now, when I say passion, I'm specifically talking about passion for the world and people. Sometimes, it's so easy to get caught up in our own lives that we forget there is a whole world out there that needs our help. As teens who love God, we must also care about who and what God loves. But to do that, we must first learn about who and what God loves.

Generally speaking, would you consider yourself a passionate person? Are there any **issues**—whether political, personal, or related to social justice—that you care deeply about? (It's okay if there aren't!)

___

___

___

___

• ◆ •

If someone asked me what I was passionate about a few years ago, I would've said nothing. As sad as it is to say, nothing tugged at my heart enough to make me want to care and make a difference. I probably would've just said I was passionate about volleyball.

I wanted to be like my friends who had something specific they cared about. I had friends who were passionate about the **environment**, friends who cared about **improving education**, and others who simply wanted to **change the world**. I always wished I had that desire.

Even though I wanted to *want* to change the world, **I couldn't find a desire like that in my heart**.

I always wondered why that was. Well, here's what I learned about passion:

> **Passion can only come from a place of love.**

To have the capacity to be passionate, you must have some foundation of love to begin with. When I was younger, I wasn't the kind and bubbly person I am today. I was the opposite—I shut people out. I didn't have a lot of love to give to other people, let alone to the issues and problems the world was facing.

It was only when I formed a relationship with God that I formed a foundation of love. From this foundation of love rooted in God, I gained the capacity to feel passion and care about people and issues outside of myself.

> As I got to know God better, I found myself caring about what God cares about and disliking things that aren't pleasing to God. **It was through God and knowing what He was passionate about that I found my passions.** But in order to care about what God cares about, you need to learn about God's heart and character. **You need to know God just like you would know a friend.**

What are some issues/people you think God really cares about? If God had an Instagram page, what kinds of people and accounts would He follow? What posts would He like? What would He post and share about?

_____
_____
_____
_____
_____

There are probably a million different things we could list. Even in Scripture, we could name one issue after another, one person after another that God deeply cares about. We will look at just three different verses that describe some of God's heart and passions. With each verse you read, consider what it says about who God loves.

Psalm 34:18

"The Lord is close to the brokenhearted and saves those who are crushed in spirit."

What does this verse say about who God loves?

_____
_____
_____
_____

What does this verse say about who God cares for?

_____
_____
_____

Luke 6:27-28

"But to you who are listening I say: Love your enemies, do good to those who hate you, bless those who curse you, pray for those who mistreat you."

> **1 John 3:17**
>
> "If anyone has material possessions and sees a brother or sister in need but has no pity on them, how can the love of God be in that person?"

What does this verse say about who God wants to help?

_____

_____

_____

The more you read your Bible, the more you get to know who God is. **Getting to know God is truly like getting to know a friend.** Think about it. Suppose you had a friend and they were very passionate about helping homeless people because her family used to be homeless. Wouldn't you start caring more about the issue of homelessness? Wouldn't your heart grow an aching for homeless people because of your friends' care for them?

As it should be with God.

If God's heart aches for something, it should also ache our heart. We should care about the brokenhearted, poor, people in need, and even our enemies. Why? **Because God cares for them and loves them.**

Now, there are obviously too many issues and people in the world for you to invest in *all* of them. That's why God has placed certain convictions in your heart towards **one or a few particular issues and people groups**. If He hasn't yet, pray that God would place a specific conviction in you. Better yet, read through your Bible, learn more about God's passions, and see what God highlights for you.

What is the group/issue/problem that you feel God has placed specifically on **your** heart?

_____

_____

_____

> For me, it's **helping youth come to know Jesus**. Because of my experience of finding God so radically as a teenager, God placed a burning desire in my heart to help other teenagers come to know Him as well. However, recently, I've also felt a call to pursue the global side of ministry. This past fall, I traveled to Washington, D.C., to intern at Bread for the World—a Christian advocacy organization fighting to end hunger in the U.S. and around the world.

God has a **different calling** for every person based on their talents and personality. God might take you far from where you are or keep you close to home. God might give you a vision to help millions of people, or God might give you the heart to help just a few in a mighty way.

No matter what passion God gives you, He wants you to pursue it wholeheartedly.

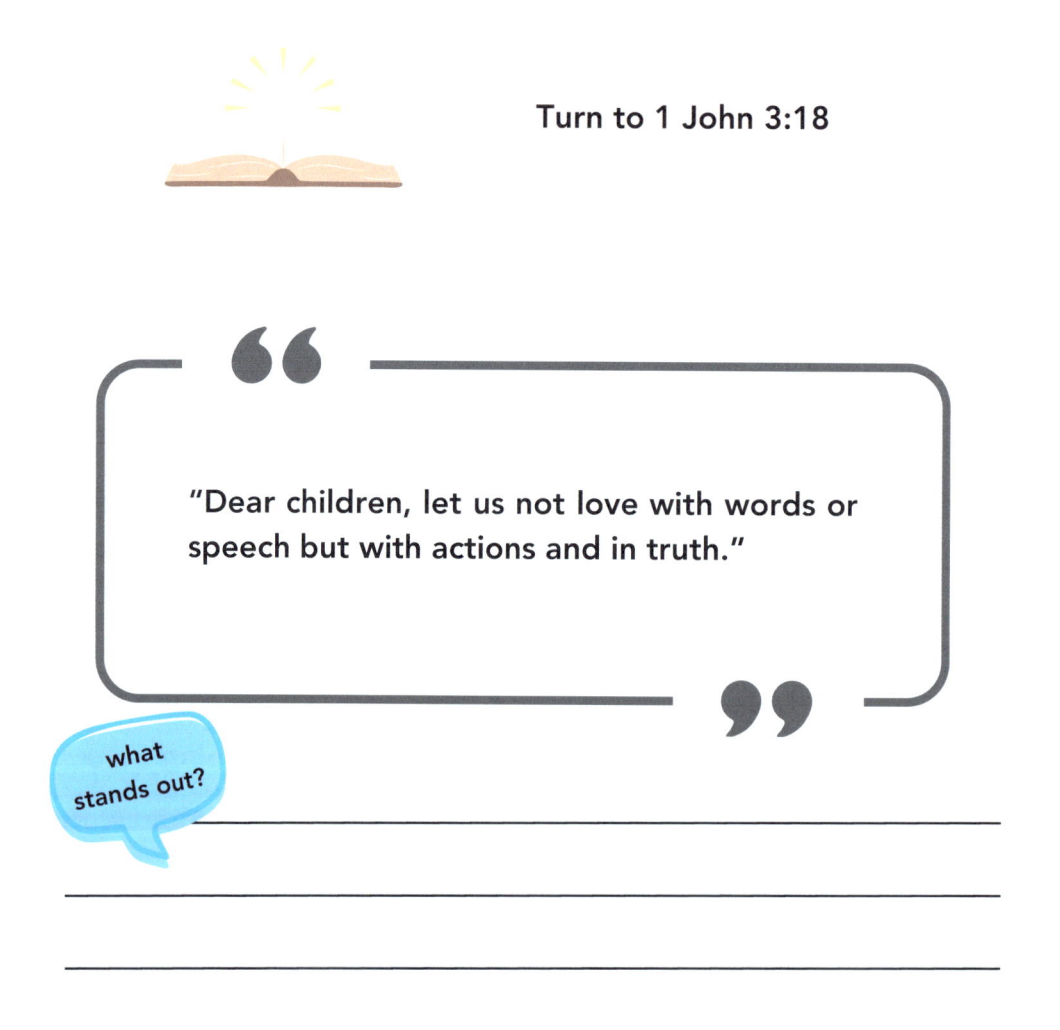

Turn to 1 John 3:18

> "Dear children, let us not love with words or speech but with actions and in truth."

what stands out?

_____
_____
_____

We can't stand back when there is a **whole world** that needs our help. God has gifted each of us with unique skills, dreams, and passions to serve the world and His people.

God calls us to go out and bring change, healing, comfort, assistance, joy, and peace to His world - but that can only be done through our **"yes"** to God.

This week's memory verse is **1 John 3:18** or any of the three other verses we looked at (**Psalms 34:18**, **Luke 6:27-28**, **1 John 3:17**). Choose the one that resonates with you the most and will help you as you pursue love and justice for Jesus. My favorite is 1 John 3:18.

"Dear children, let us not love with words or speech but with actions and in truth."

PRAYER REQUESTS

NOTES

DATE:

Recite 1 John 3:18 or any of the other 3 verses

WEEK 7
FINDING HUMILITY

Can you believe we're almost done with this study? Welcome to finding humility. Pride is one of the hardest sins to overcome. It's not like lying or cheating, which are sins you can intentionally avoid. Pride is deeper and much more complex. Pride is a heart problem, and it shows up even when you try your hardest for it not to.

> **Take for example:** You're doing community service work, which is amazing to do, right? Yet, when you think about how amazing the work you're doing is, the first thought that enters your mind is: "I'm such a good person for doing this." I'm not saying this is a horrible thought to have, but I give this example to show that **pride can pop up anywhere and everywhere.**

Think about it. Even if I were to ask: Do you consider yourself a humble person? It seems as though to say "yes," even if you really are humble, is prideful to say about yourself. See what I mean? **Anything – even and especially good things – can turn into pride.**

Do you think you struggle with pride? What areas of your life do you struggle with pride the most?

_____

_____

_____

_____

For me, my area of pride was my **friendships**—specifically, who I chose to be friends with and who I chose not to. Being the captain of my volleyball team, having good grades in school, and being very busy and hardworking, I didn't like hanging out with people who I felt weren't as "good" as me.

It sounds bad to say, but at the time, I wanted my friends to be just as busy, hardworking, and accomplished as I was. **I was so proud of my talents and work ethic that it got in the way of my ability to be kind, open, and a good person to everyone I interacted with, not just those I wanted to be good to.**

> According to Oxford Languages, **pride is "a feeling of deep pleasure or satisfaction derived from one's own achievements… or from qualities or possessions that are widely admired."** Honestly, this definition of pride doesn't make it seem inherently bad. It's good to find satisfaction in your achievements and to be confident in the qualities people praise you for.

However, pride becomes a sin when you soak and bask in your "greatness." It becomes bad when you start thinking that you're better than others, that you're always right, and that things must always go your way. **At its worst, pride is thinking you know better than God—it's thinking you're above God.**

That leads us to what this meeting is truly about: **humility**. Following Jesus requires humility. You cannot follow Him without it because when you find God, you realize who He is compared to who you are. Even if I thought I was the world's greatest volleyball player and student, **God is the King of the universe**. If you ask me, that's not even a comparison.

It's humbling to realize you are just a small part of this amazing world God has designed. It's humbling to understand your life here on earth is not only short but also just a blip in what has happened and what is yet to come. **Humility is key to our relationship with our God.**

But before we talk more about humility in Jesus, how would you define humility? What makes someone a **humble person**?

_____

_____

_____

_____

_____

Now, I have a friend who I always thought was really humble. This friend constantly downplays their strengths, rejects compliments, and says "sorry" about everything. Initially, I thought this friend of mine was just extremely humble. Yet, I've learned there is a difference between **worldly humility** and **humble confidence** in God.

Is this type of **"worldly humility"** familiar to you? Do you have friends like this? Are you this person yourself? (Turn to the next page for a definition of worldly humility)

_____

_____

_____

_____

_____

I don't want us to get trapped in worldly humility. Worldly humility downplays our strengths, rejects encouragement, and always puts the blame 100% on us. This type of humility isn't just the absence of pride – **it's diminishing our personhood.**

Rather, **humble confidence—or humility in Jesus—is when we know where we stand before God, but in reverence and obedience, we acknowledge and display the gifts He has given us.** It's knowing we are beautiful, wonderful, and unique, but that we ultimately belong to Jesus and the body of Christ.

Turn to 1 Corinthians 12:17-20

> "If the whole body were an eye, where would the sense of hearing be? If the whole body were an ear, where would the sense of smell be? But in fact God has placed the parts in the body, every one of them, just as he wanted them to be. If they were all one part, where would the body be? **As it is, there are many parts, but one body.**"

1 Corinthians 12 talks about how every member of the body of Christ is unique and helpful. However, it also teaches the importance of recognizing that every member is meant to support the body of God, not just themselves.

What stands out to you in this passage? Does this passage or what we learned **change** your initial definition of humility?

_____

_____

_____

_____

I recommend reading the whole passage of **1 Corinthians 12:12-31**. I think it's cool how the passage celebrates our uniqueness and importance while also reminding us that we are all part of one body. To fully support the head of the body (which is God), we must confidently and purposefully play our part well. **If we play our part down, the whole body suffers.**

We are all reflections of God. We are His image-bearers. If that is who we are, **shouldn't we shine?** Shouldn't we reflect the splendor, beauty, and awesomeness of our God? Shouldn't we fully be who God has magnificently woven us together to be?

How can you practice **humble confidence**? Do you need to work more on humility or confidence?

_____

_____

_____

_____

_____

If you've followed Jesus long enough, you've probably heard the phrase: **"You must decrease so God can increase."** While this statement is true, it isn't complete. We must decrease, but we must make sure not to diminish ourselves to nothing. **We must remember that making God bigger in our lives does not reduce our value or worth in any way.** Yes, it decreases your desire to live for yourself and be your own God, but never should you feel like you must become nothing.

God created you intentionally, purposefully, and beautifully. God took His time to handcraft and design you with the careful touch of His fingers. Sometimes, we think making ourselves nothing to make God everything is how God would be the most glorified.

In reality, how can we glorify God when we are **invalidating** and **hiding** the unique person that God created us to be?

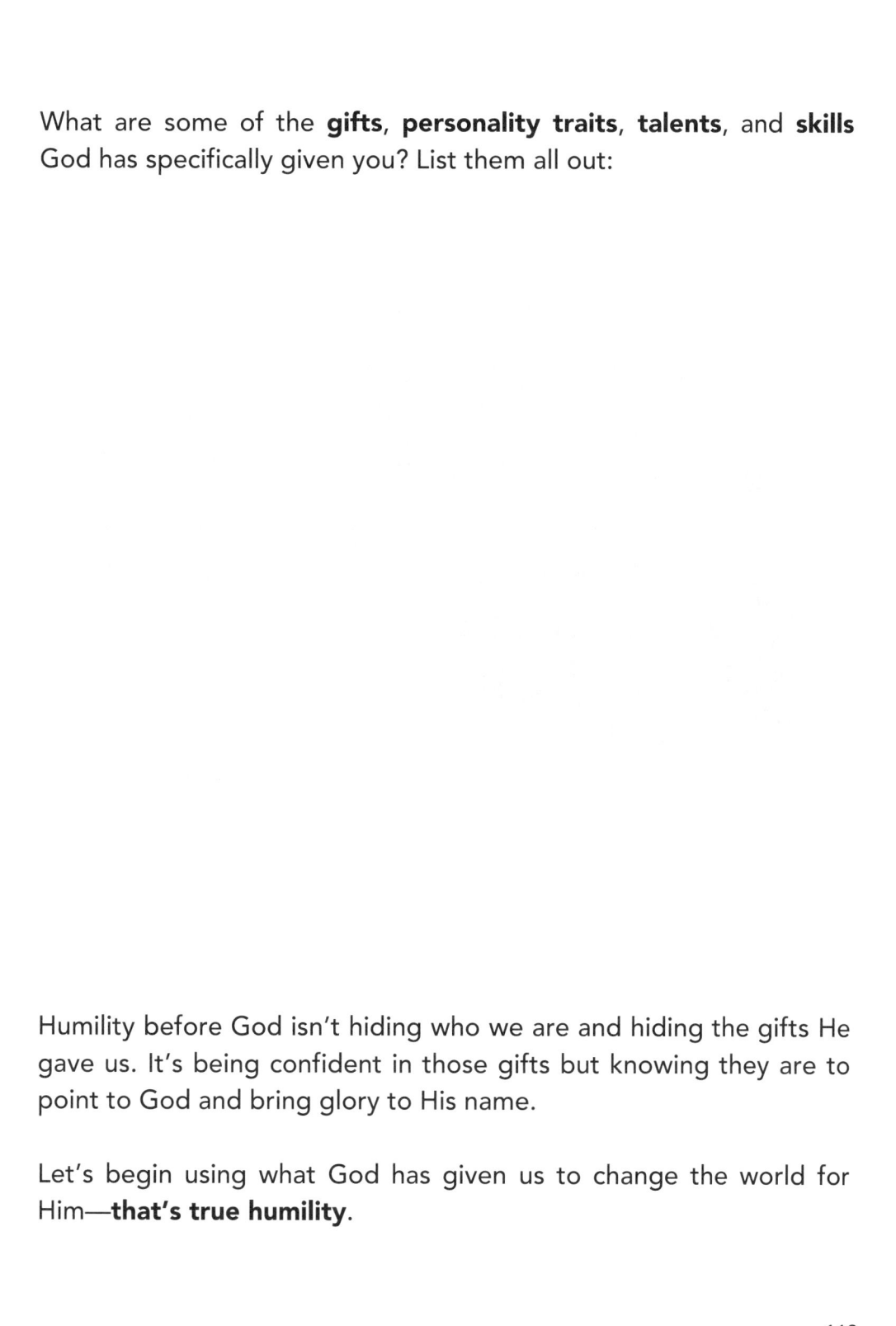

What are some of the **gifts**, **personality traits**, **talents**, and **skills** God has specifically given you? List them all out:

Humility before God isn't hiding who we are and hiding the gifts He gave us. It's being confident in those gifts but knowing they are to point to God and bring glory to His name.

Let's begin using what God has given us to change the world for Him—**that's true humility**.

These girls amaze me with all the God-given gifts they possess. **Noelle** cares so deeply about people and always wants to help. **Reese** has one of the brightest and joyful spirits ever. **Olivia** represents beauty both inside and out. **Peyton** is so gentle and kind. **Kayla** is brave, bold, and incredibly wise.

This week's verses are **1 Corinthians 12:18-20**. As we memorize these verses throughout the week, let's remember that both humility and confidence are required to fully serve God and the body of Christ.

"But in fact God has placed the parts in the body, every one of them, just as he wanted them to be. If they were all one part, where would the body be? As it is, there are many parts, but one body."

If you're in a group, your leader will test you **on all your Bible verses from the past seven weeks** next week—so make sure you review them! You can write down the verses you memorized on page 121 to have them all in one place.

PRAYER REQUESTS

NOTES

DATE:

Recite 1 Corinthians 12:18-20

WEEK 8
FINDING ME

Wow, it's already our final meeting! I'm so proud of how much you've accomplished through this study. Everything we've covered thus far has ultimately led us closer to finding you. I hope that as we end with this last session, you can walk away with a deeper and fuller understanding of who God is and what that means about who you are.

NOTES

MEMORY VERSE CHALLENGE

Write down the verses you chose to memorize for each week and recite them out loud to your group leader!

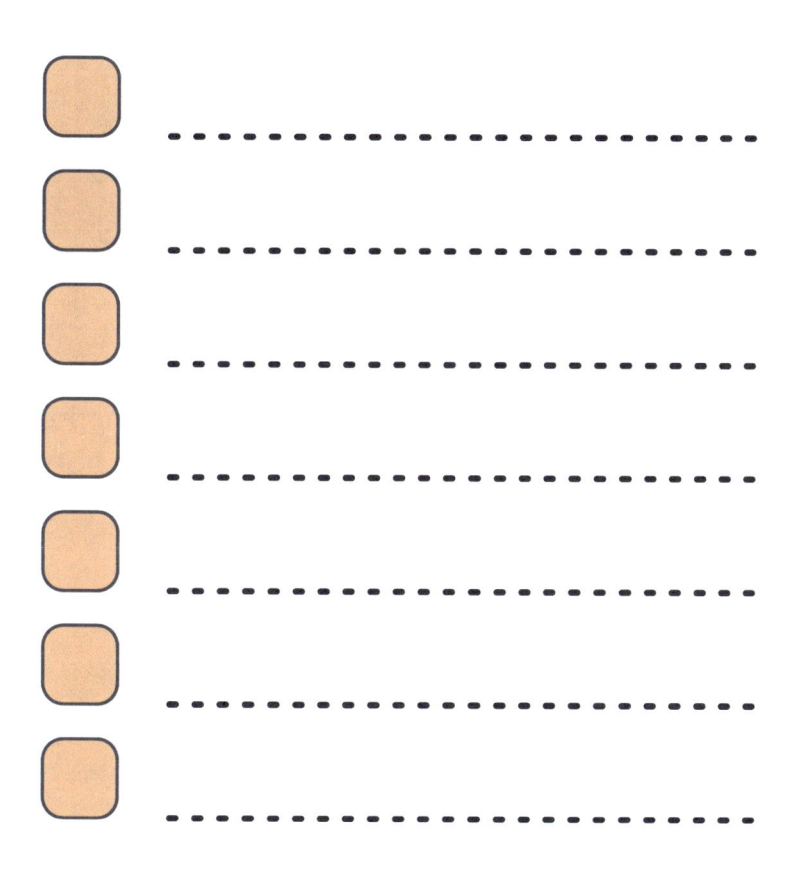

- [ ] ....
- [ ] ....
- [ ] ....
- [ ] ....
- [ ] ....
- [ ] ....
- [ ] ....

The questions and ideas we tackled these past two months weren't easy, but they were so necessary and crucial for us to talk about. **Identity. Confidence. Patience. Passion. Purpose. Humility**. We've talked about some very fundamental values. However, there are so many more values, attributes, and qualities I hope you find in your lifetime besides just these. I hope you find joy, kindness, friendship, love, forgiveness, self-control, and all the other good fruits of the Spirit.

Yet, what I hope you've taken away is that all these good things can only be found in one place. People spend a lifetime trying to figure out who they are. **I'm telling you right now that *you* can only be found in Jesus.**

Here's the me I found in Jesus through all of this. I wrote this reflection of who I am through Jesus in my book back when I was 16. While you read my reflection, I want you to start thinking about what you would write—I'm going to ask you to write one right after I share mine:

> Before I found God, I saw myself simply as a shy, closed-off, and insecure teenager. I have been set free from those chains. Through God, I have come to know the truth about who I am. **I have found me.** I have found the me who loves people with an overflowing love. The me who makes sure everyone feels **welcomed**, **included**, and **accepted**. The me who sees the girl sitting by herself at lunch and goes to **sit** with her. The me who **boldly** tells people the gospel as I walk down the street. The me who goes overboard with people's birthdays, because I want people to feel **celebrated** and **cherished**. The me who **smiles** and **laughs** in every moment I get. The me who puts **both** hands up in worship. The me who **isn't afraid** to pursue my dreams that seem too big because of the God I believe in who's bigger. The me who **so badly** wants to see my generation saved. The me who **risks my reputation** and people liking me for the sake of making Christ's name known to the world. The me who is **willing to drop everything** and follow Jesus… The me who has absolutely fallen in **love** with Jesus. **This is the me I have found through finding God.** (pg. 145-146)

This is the me that is the result of being set free and transformed by Jesus. Nothing I wrote about who I am could exist without Jesus and what He has done in my life. **It's the me who's only possible because of Him.**

Now, I want **you** to write about the person you are only through Jesus. Write about the person you are *because* of Jesus. What does Jesus make you that you couldn't be on your own?

_____

_____

_____

_____

_____

_____

_____

_____

_____

_____

Choosing to be the you that you just wrote about is a **daily choice**. Sin, brokenness, and emptiness will still exist in your life. Being in relationship with God doesn't mean you're exempt from this reality. What it does mean, though, is that you can choose every morning to be the person God changed you to be.

Turn to Psalm 23

This is one of my favorite Psalms because this passage is essentially **David's answer** to the question we just answered. This is who David is only through Jesus:

"The Lord is my shepherd, **I lack nothing**. He makes me **lie down** in green pastures, he **leads** me beside quiet water, he **refreshes** my soul. He **guides** me along the right paths for his name's sake. Even though I walk through the darkest valley, **I will fear no evil**, for you are with me; your rod and your staff, they **comfort** me. You **prepare** a table before me in the presence of my enemies. You **anoint** my head with oil; my cup **overflows.** Surely your goodness and love will follow me all the days of my life, and **I will dwell in the house of the Lord forever.**"

REFLECTION QUESTIONS

For the bulk of today's meeting, I want you to spend time with your group and discuss these **reflection questions!**

What was the topic that helped you the most? Identity? Confidence? Purpose?

_____

_____

_____

_____

What is the biggest insight you gained/learned through this study? What will you take away?

_____

_____

_____

_____

Has your relationship with God grown through this Bible study? How has it grown? How has it changed?

_____

_____

_____

_____

_____

⭐ ⭐ ⭐ ⭐ ⭐ ⭐ ⭐ ⭐ ⭐ ⭐

Thank you for doing this Bible study and choosing to commit to it. I've been praying constantly over this study and for you. I wish I could be in person to have gone through this study with you, but I trust that your leaders and God have spoken into your life and convicted you through this guide.

I hope the end of these meetings marks the **beginning** of a new journey for you with God. I hope you continue to draw close to Him, dive into His Word, and constantly gather with your friends to engage in community and fellowship. **I hope you never stop finding God and finding you.**

I know our memory verse challenge is over, but I'll still leave you with **Psalms 23:6** to memorize. Let this be a reminder that God is with you **always and forever**.

> "Surely your goodness and love will follow me all the days of my life, and I will dwell in the house of the Lord forever."

ONE MORE THING!

> This study is meant to be passed down after you've completed it. Since you have made your way through as a participant in this study, you now get to be the **leader** of one. I want you to take on 2-4 friends or younger peers and invest in them for another eight weeks. **You are now a disciple-maker who gets to help lead others to Jesus—how awesome is that?**

Also, if you're hesitant to lead, co-lead with a friend! This study was designed to be simple to follow and lead. Take on this challenge together—I promise you it will be so worth it.

Your new group:

_____

_____

_____

_____

CONGRATS ON FINISHING! WE ARE SO PROUD OF YOU.

"Therefore go and make disciples of all nations, baptizing them in the name of the Father and of the Son and of the Holy Spirit, and teaching them to obey everything I have commanded you. And surely I am with you always, to the very end of the age." – Matthew 28:19-20

NOTES

ABOUT THE AUTHOR

Izzy Koo is a college student at Pepperdine University dedicated to leading youth to Christ. Izzy met God radically in her sophomore year of high school and, since then, has committed her life to serving God and others. In 2021, Izzy released her first book, "Finding God, Finding Me," where she shares her story of meeting God as an ordinary teenager. Izzy is regularly invited to speak at churches, youth retreats, and conferences across the country to share her unique and powerful testimony. She hopes to pursue youth ministry in the future and continue to use writing, speaking, and mentorship to transform lives through faith.

Alongside her studies, Izzy currently serves as the NextGen Coordinator at the Asian American Christian Collaborative (AACC), where she leads efforts to invest in the next generation of Asian American Christians.

Izzy loves her family and adores her two younger sisters, Olivia and Noelle. In her free time, she loves to play volleyball and pickleball with her friends, meet new people, and watch Korean dramas.

You can keep up with Izzy on Instagram at izzy_koo. You can also follow her on her blog at www.mywaytofindingme.com.

Made in the USA
Columbia, SC
01 July 2024